Respecting the Contributions of
Disabled Americans

Sloan MacRae

PowerKiDS press

New York

Published in 2013 by The Rosen Publishing Group, Inc.
29 East 21st Street, New York, NY 10010

First Edition

Editor: Jennifer Way
Book Design: Erica Clendening and Ashley Drago
Layout Design: Andrew Povolny

Photo Credits: Cover, p. 16 Adam Pretty/Getty Images; p. 5 iStockphoto/Thinkstock; p. 6 SW Productions/Photodisc/Getty Images; p. 7 Moodboard/The Agency Collection/Getty Images; p. 9 Barros & Barros/The Image Bank/ Getty Images; pp. 10, 11 Andy Nelson/Christian Science Monitor/Getty Images; p. 12 Hulton Archive/Getty Images; p. 13 Hemera/Thinkstock; p. 14 Central Press/Hulton Archive/Getty Images; p. 15 Jeff Fusco/Getty p. 17 Chris Hyde/Getty Images; p. 19 George Doyle/Stockbyte/Thinkstock; p. 20 Tom Williams/CQ-Roll Call Group/Getty Images; p. 21 Andrew H. Walker/Getty Images; p. 22 Realistic Reflections/Getty Images

Library of Congress Cataloging-in-Publication Data

MacRae, Sloan.
  Respecting the contributions of disabled Americans / by Sloan MacRae. — 1st ed.
     p. cm. — (Stop bullying now!)
  Includes index.
  ISBN 978-1-4488-7445-3 (library binding) — ISBN 978-1-4488-7518-4 (pbk.) —
  ISBN 978-1-4488-7592-4 (6-pack)
  1. People with disabilities—United States—Juvenile literature. 2. Bullying—Juvenile literature. I. Title.
  HV1553.M34 2013
  305.9'080973—dc23
                                                2012004240

Manufactured in the United States of America

CPSIA Compliance Information: Batch #SW12PK: For Further Information contact Rosen Publishing, New York, New York at 1-800-237-9932

Contents

What Is a Disability?

A **disability** is a condition that makes it difficult or impossible for a person to do something. When you think of disabilities, you might think of a **physical disability**, but vision and hearing **impairments** are disabilities, too. People with **intellectual disabilities** have difficulty learning and living independently. Sometimes people are born with a disability. Other times a person may become disabled from an injury or an illness.

People with disabilities have dealt with **discrimination** and bullying to get the rights that all Americans deserve. This book will tell you more about the contributions disabled Americans have made to this country.

Being unable to walk is a physical disability. Many people who cannot walk need to use wheelchairs. Some disabilities are harder to see than this one, though. About five percent of children age 5 to 17 have some type of disability.

What Is Bullying?

People who are bullies hurt or threaten other people. Bullies might also exclude a person, call him names, or spread rumors about him. Bullying can happen online as well as face-to-face.

Bullies pick on people they see as different. It is important that schools not tolerate bullying and stop it when it happens.

Down syndrome is an intellectual disability that a person is born with. Children with disabilities are more likely to be bullied than other children.

People who are seen as different are sometimes the target of bullies. Bullies might pick on a disabled girl because she looks or acts differently from other kids. Bullying is wrong, and it is important for everyone at school to know that it can and should be stopped. Parents, teachers, and other trusted adults can help if you or someone at your school is being bullied.

Disability Rights

Throughout history, people with disabilities of all types have faced discrimination. They were kept out of school and denied jobs. Sometimes families placed disabled family members in hospital-like **institutions**, where they spent the rest of their lives.

Things began to change in the twentieth century, when people began to speak out for equal rights for disabled Americans. One area in which people have worked is to make things **accessible**, or able to be used by, people with disabilities. Today, groups like the American Association of People with Disabilities work to promote equal treatment for Americans with disabilities.

Today 99 percent of public buses have ramps or lifts that make them accessible to people with disabilities. This is because people worked for disability rights.

Gallaudet University

Gallaudet University, in Washington, D.C., was founded in 1864. It is the world's only university where all of its classes and services are designed for students with hearing impairments. The school was named for Thomas Hopkins Gallaudet. He was an educator of students with hearing impairments who helped develop **American Sign Language**.

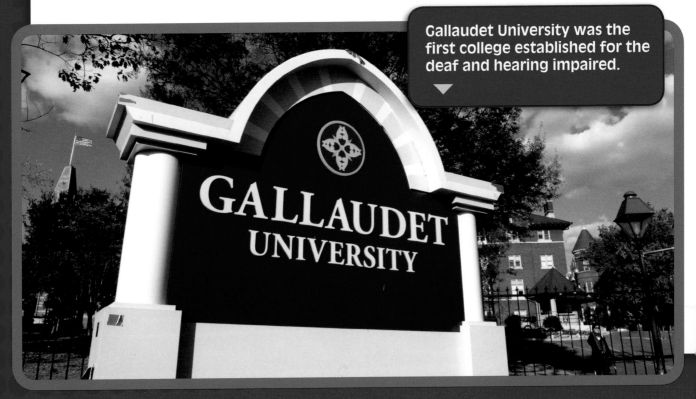

Gallaudet University was the first college established for the deaf and hearing impaired.

Here is a Gallaudet student using sign language to talk to a newspaper reporter about events at her school. ▶

Since its founding, Gallaudet University has made higher education more accessible to people who are deaf or hard of hearing. It has also helped students understand their rights, find jobs, and contribute to their communities.

Helen Keller

Helen Keller was born in 1880. She became ill at 19 months old, and that illness left her unable to hear or see. In 1887, her parents hired a teacher named Ann Sullivan to work with Helen. Sullivan helped Helen learn to communicate through finger spelling and writing. She also learned to read **Braille** and to speak. She went on to college and graduated in 1904.

Helen Keller lost her sight and hearing before she learned to talk. Her achievements made people think differently about what people with disabilities could do.

This picture shows the signs for the letters of the alphabet. Using these signs, people can finger spell words and communicate with people with hearing impairments.

Keller spent her adult life speaking and writing about improving the education and living conditions of people with disabilities, women's rights, and other social issues. She continued her work until a few years before her death in 1968.

Franklin Delano Roosevelt is the only president to have served more than two terms. He was re-elected three times and died at the beginning of his fourth term.

Franklin Delano Roosevelt was born in 1882. In 1921, an illness left him **paralyzed** from the waist down. In private, he used a wheelchair. In public, he took care to keep the spotlight on his work, rather than his disability. Roosevelt founded a charity to fight the illness that caused his disability. This charity later became the March of Dimes. Today the March of Dimes works to prevent **birth defects**, many of which cause disabilities.

Roosevelt was elected president in 1932. He led the United States through the Great Depression and World War II. Roosevelt died while in office in 1945.

Max Cleland (1942-)

Max Cleland served in the US Army and lost both legs and his right arm in the Vietnam War. Cleland went on to serve in the US Senate from 1997 until 2003. He now helps run the American Battle Monuments Commission, a government agency that builds and maintains memorials for American veterans.

The Paralympic Games and the Special Olympics

The Paralympic Games and Special Olympics are organizations that allow people with disabilities to compete in a wide range of sports. Eunice Kennedy Shriver founded the Special Olympics in 1968 to allow people with intellectual disabilities to play sports.

The US Paralympic Women's Wheelchair Basketball Team won the gold medal in the 2008 Paralympic Games in Beijing, China.

The Paralympics gets its name from the Greek word *pará*, which means "alongside," because the games are held alongside the Olympic Games.

The Paralympic Games are held after each Olympic Games in the same city. The Paralympics began in 1960 to allow athletes with physical disabilities to compete in sports. Many of the first Paralympic athletes were veterans who had become disabled in war. The Paralympic Games were created to focus on the participants' athletic achievements, rather than on their disabilities.

For many years, children with disabilities did not get the free public education that all American kids have a right to. In the 1970s, only one-fifth of children with disabilities were attending a public school. Many of these kids were in institutions where they had no education. Others were in public schools that kept them apart and offered little education.

The Individuals with Disabilities Education Act, or IDEA, is a 1990 law. It requires public schools to create education plans for students with disabilities that affect their abilities to participate at school.

By 2006, more than six million American children had access to educational services through IDEA.

Americans with Disabilities Act

ADA:
Advancing Equal Rights
for All Americans

In 2010, Congressman Jim Langevin, of Rhode Island, spoke at an event honoring the twentieth anniversary of the Americans with Disabilities Act. Langevin became disabled following an accident when he was 16.

Everyone in the United States has a right to use public services and to not face discrimination when looking for a job. These kinds of rights are called civil rights.

Congress passed a law in 1990 called the Americans with Disabilities Act. This civil rights law made it illegal to deny services to people with disabilities. This means adding things such as wheelchair ramps, Braille materials, and special parking spaces. Some cities have stoplights that make sounds so that vision-impaired people can safely cross the street. This law makes sure that people with disabilities have access to the same services as their fellow Americans.

Michael J. Fox (1961-)

Michael J. Fox is an Emmy-Award-winning actor who was diagnosed with Parkinson's disease in 1991. This is a disabling movement disorder that gets worse over time. Fox became an activist for research for Parkinson's treatments and started the Michael J. Fox Foundation to raise money for Parkinson's research.

Respecting Americans with Disabilities

Everyone has different abilities and struggles. Everyone has the right to an education and the opportunity to participate in society.

It is wrong to bully or discriminate against people with disabilities. If you hear someone saying mean things about people with disabilities, you should remind him that everyone deserves respect. You can even share some of the important facts you have learned about the contributions that people with disabilities have made to the United States.

Learning to respect what makes each person different and understanding that everyone has feelings is important to building a community that includes everyone.

Glossary

accessible (ik-SEH-suh-bel) Able to be used or reached.

American Sign Language (uh-MER-uh-kun SYN LANG-gwij) A language for the deaf that uses hand movements and signs.

birth defects (BURTH DEE-fekts) Problems that are present at birth.

Braille (BRAYL) An alphabet of raised dots that blind people use to read and write.

disability (dis-uh-BIH-luh-tee) A condition such as blindness that makes someone unable to do certain things.

discrimination (dis-krih-muh-NAY-shun) Treating a person badly or unfairly just because he or she is different.

impairments (im-PER-ments) Things that are damaged or worse than is common.

institutions (in-stuh-TOO-shunz) Established organizations or foundations, such as schools or hospitals.

intellectual disabilities (in-teh-LEK-chuh-wul dis-uh-BIH-luh-teez) Limits in the way people's brains work. It means that people have trouble with many skills.

paralyzed (PER-uh-lyzd) To have lost feeling or movement.

physical disability (FIH-zih-kul dis-uh-BIH-luh-tee) An impairment that limits the way certain parts of the body work and how they move.

Index

Websites

Due to the changing nature of Internet links, PowerKids Press has developed an online list of websites related to the subject of this book. This site is updated regularly. Please use this link to access the list:

www.powerkidslinks.com/sbn/disab/